A Life Well Lived

OTHER BOOKS BY THE AUTHOR

Books for Adults

Active Spirituality

Bedside Blessings

Behold . . . The Man!

The Bride

Come Before Winter

Compassion: Showing We Care in a
  Careless World

The Darkness and the Dawn

David: A Man of Passion and Destiny

Day by Day

Dear Graduate

Dropping Your Guard

Elijah: A Man of Heroism and Humility

Encourage Me

Encouragement for Life

Esther: A Woman of Strength and Dignity

Fascinating Stories Forgotten Lives

The Finishing Touch

Five Meaningful Minutes a Day

Flying Closer to the Flame

For Those Who Hurt

Getting Through the Tough Stuff

God's Provision

The Grace Awakening

The Grace Awakening Devotional

Great Attitudes!

Great Days with Great Lives

Growing Deep in the Christian Life

Growing Strong in the Seasons of Life

Growing Wise in Family Life

Hand Me Another Brick

Home: Where Life Makes Up Its Mind

Hope Again

Improving Your Serve

Intimacy with the Almighty

Job: A Man of Heroic Endurance

Joseph: A Man of Integrity and Forgiveness

Killing Giants, Pulling Thorns

Laugh Again

Leadership: Influence That Inspires

Living Above the Level of Mediocrity

Living Beyond the Daily Grind, Books I
  and II

The Living Insights Study Bible, general
  editor

Living on the Ragged Edge

Living on the Ragged Edge
  Workbook

Make Up Your Mind

Man to Man

Marriage: From Surviving to Thriving

Moses: A Man of Selfless Dedication

The Mystery of God's Will

Parenting: From Surviving to Thriving

Paul: A Man of Grace and Grit

The Quest for Character

Recovery: When Healing Takes Time

The Road to Armageddon

Sanctity of Life

A Life Well Lived

Charles R. Swindoll

Thomas Nelson
Since 1798

NASHVILLE   DALLAS   MEXICO CITY   RIO DE JANEIRO

Published in Nashville, Tennessee, by Thomas Nelson. Thomas Nelson is a registered trademark of Thomas Nelson, Inc.

Published in association with Yates & Yates, LLP, Attorneys and Counselors, Orange, California.

Thomas Nelson, Inc., titles may be purchased in bulk for educational, business, fund-raising, or sales promotional use. For information, please e-mail SpecialMarkets@ThomasNelson.com.

Unless otherwise noted scripture quotations are taken from the New American Standard Bible. © The Lockman Foundation 1960, 1962, 1963, 1968, 1971, 1972, 1973, 1975, 1977, 1995. Used by permission.

Scripture quotations marked MSG are taken from *The Message* by Eugene H. Peterson. © 1993, 1994, 1995, 1996, 2000. Used by permission of NavPress Publishing Group. All rights reserved.

ISBN 978-1-4002-7856-5 (SE)
                Library of Congress Cataloging-in-Publication Data

Swindoll, Charles R.
    A life well lived / Charles R. Swindoll.
        p. cm.
    Includes bibliographical references.
    ISBN: 978-0-8499-0189-8 (hardcover)
    1. Christian life—Biblical teaching. 2. Bible. O.T. Micah—Criticism, inter-
pretation, etc. I. Title.
BS1615.6.C43S95 2007
248.4—dc22   2007010430
                Printed in the United States of America

        10 11 12 13 14 RRD 5 4 3 2 1

DEDICATION

It is with heartfelt gratitude for his "life well lived"
that I dedicate this volume to my longtime friend
and greatly esteemed president of Biola University,
DR. CLYDE COOK.

Throughout the years of his life he has
faithfully modeled Christlikeness in numerous roles:
an athlete, a husband, a father, a missionary, an educator.
And for the last twenty-five years he has
led the faculty and shepherded the students of Biola
"according to the integrity of his heart,
and guided them with his skillful hands."
He exemplifies the message of this book
better than most.

TABLE OF CONTENTS

He has told you, O man, what is good;
And what does the LORD require of you
But to do justice, to love kindness,
And to walk humbly with your God?

—MICAH 6:8

Introduction

"It Was the Best of Times, It Was the Worst of Times..."

As I reflect on the familiar words of Charles Dickens, I recall one of the best and worst times of my life. July 1, 1994, began a period that I can best describe as a long, cold winter—a stark, lonely season during which I found myself without all the things that gave me comfort, purpose, meaning, and identity. It helped a little that I entered this season willingly. It was a necessary transition from a very successful, almost twenty-three years in Fullerton, California, to an uncertain future in Dallas, Texas. I never doubted that I was where the Lord would have me and I knew it would be difficult, but I never imagined just how much it would challenge my character and stretch my faith. I felt more than lonely. I felt alone.

I was living in a small apartment over a friend's garage while pouring myself into my new duties as president of Dallas Theological Seminary, the institution that had launched me into ministry thirty-one years earlier. The world of academic theology, while strange to me, was stimulating. Those with whom I worked could not have been more gracious and kind . . . but nothing was familiar. It would be another two years before we could move the headquarters of Insight for Living from California to Texas, so Cynthia had to divide her time between Anaheim and Dallas. That left me with a lot of solitude, something I typically enjoy. But this was far more than I had anticipated or wanted. I was separated from all of my children and grandchildren for the first time since they were born. The deep friendships I had cultivated for twenty-three years were fifteen hundred miles away. The home we had lived in and enjoyed belonged to someone else, and the ministry that had given me such joy and fulfillment was now only a memory. Moreover, I was a shepherd without sheep. That loss kept me on my face before God.

In those best/worst seasons of life, when the cold of winter prunes us back to the stump, we can do little more than mourn our losses, cling to an uncertain hope of spring, and allow God to strengthen our roots. And in the quietness, I believe God invites us to put our deepest questions before Him. In my new beginning, one of those questions was, what do You expect of me?

My desire was not to discover how to gain God's pleasure. Those of us who have placed our trust in Jesus Christ need to rest in the sure knowledge that God is immensely pleased with us already. Christ's atoning death and triumphant resurrection have completely satisfied the Father, and now the Son's righteousness is ours. This is what He said, and I believe Him. Nevertheless, the answer to the question, what do You expect of me? holds the key to something that doesn't come automatically. It's something I must pursue: a life well lived.

I found the answer to my question in the solitude of my own little upper room during the best and worst times of my life. I discovered the answer in the words of the prophet Micah, who wrote to an affluent society in hot pursuit of all the wrong things. *What does the Lord expect of us?* He's uncompromising, but He isn't demanding. In fact, the simplicity of the answer Micah received directly from the Lord may surprise you.

Chapter 1

Doing What's Right

WE DON'T HAVE PROPHETS TODAY, AT LEAST NOT
in the strict sense of the word. Before and during the time
when the Bible was being written, prophets received revelation from God and delivered it to the people. People
knew that when a genuine prophet spoke, the message was
as good as from the lips of God Himself. The truthfulness
of the message authenticated the messenger. If a person
claimed to speak from God and gave information that
proved to be false, he or she was taken to the edge of town,
cast into a ditch, and stoned to death. So, generally speaking, the word of a prophet was considered reliable . . . at
least when the people cared to hear from God.

Micah was one of those trustworthy prophets who lived
and ministered in Judah around 700 BC. Scholars group
him among what they call "the minor prophets" because
their writings are significantly shorter than those of "the

3

major prophets," such as Isaiah, Jeremiah, and Ezekiel. This is not to suggest that any of their writings are unimportant. On the contrary, each "minor prophet" expressed profound truth in a relatively small amount of space and delivered his message at a crucial juncture in Hebrew history.

After Solomon's reign ended around 931 BC, civil war divided his kingdom into two nations, Israel to the north and Judah in the south. As Judah wavered in its faithfulness to God under the ambiguous morality of its kings, Israel consistently pursued evil. And by 722 BC, after repeated warnings by a multitude of faithful prophets, God's patience reached the end of its tether and He allowed the Assyrian Empire to invade and conquer Israel.

The brutality of the Assyrian assault had a chilling effect on the people of Judah. As their kinsmen to the north were either tortured to death or deported to places unknown, Judah experienced a renewed interest in serving the Lord. But this lasted only a few years. As Micah began to write, the awful spectacle of Israel's destruction was still fresh in his mind. He feared for his people, who had begun to behave as their brothers up north had. He saw compromise in the corruption of the priests, the selfishness of the ruling class, and the outright fabrication on the part of false prophets.

His people needed a word from God.

WHAT THE LORD DOES NOT EXPECT

Against the chorus of false prophets, Micah stood alone to deliver God's message to Judah. In the sixth chapter of his book, Micah alternately records the words of God and then responds on behalf of Judah. Speaking for God, he asks the nation Judah:

> My people, what have I done to you,
>   And how have I wearied you? Answer Me.
> Indeed, I brought you up from the land of Egypt
>   And ransomed you from the house of slavery,
>   And I sent before you Moses, Aaron and Miriam.
>
> (vv. 3–4)

Then in response, Micah represents the words of Judah before the Lord:

With what shall I come to the LORD
>> And bow myself before the God on high?
>> Shall I come to Him with burnt offerings,
>> With yearling calves?
Does the LORD take delight in thousands of rams,
>> In ten thousand rivers of oil?
>> Shall I present my firstborn for my
>>> rebellious acts,
>> The fruit of my body for the sin of my soul?

(vv. 6–7)

Take note of how the people of Judah think they must approach God. They're bargaining. They're treating the Lord like the capricious gods of Egypt, Canaan, and the idolatrous, brutal Assyrians. All false religions have at least one thing in common: they attempt to win divine favor through deeds of service or sacrifice. The people of Judah began with expressions of worship prescribed by Hebrew Law, and then expanded them to ridiculous proportions.

Shall I bring an olah? That's the Hebrew word for a burnt offering of an entire animal, from nose to tail—hide, hooves, and all. *Shall I bring an expensive animal and burn all of it before the Lord? How about several?* Then they suppose that if the Lord is pleased with that sacrifice, certainly He would be ecstatic over a massive offering. *Would He be pleased if I offered whole herds of livestock? What if I topped it off with multiple barrels of expensive olive oil? Or even better, ten thousand rivers of oil! Is that what He wants from us?*

Their bargaining doesn't stop there. *What if I sacrifice my precious firstborn child on the altar? Will God then be pleased?*

Their bartering for the Lord's favor moved from regular worship, to exaggerated reverence, to hyperbole, then blasphemy. That's the problem with works-based religion. You can never sacrifice enough, work hard enough, pray long enough, or bow low enough to earn God's pleasure. And the tragic irony of Judah's cosmic bribery is that the Lord valued nothing they offered. Human sacrifice is an affront to His character, and attempts to buy His love assumes He is cheap.

Unfortunately, this bartering for the Lord's favor has never ended. Ask people today what it takes to please God, and almost without exception, they'll begin a long list of good deeds. The rise of the "word-faith" movement is all the proof we need that pagan bribery is alive and well. Health-and-wealth hucksters now dominate the airwaves, convincing multitudes of suffering people that if only they will "plant a seed" (that is, a substantial donation to a particular ministry), God will favor them with a bountiful harvest of money, expensive possessions, healing, success, or love . . . whatever they long for.

Take a good, hard look at your own relationship with the Lord. As you review your prayers and examine your motivation for giving to Him, what fuels your actions? Fear of God's wrath? Jesus bore the wrath of God for all humankind. If you are a believer in Jesus Christ, there isn't any left for you. Are you trying to make up for past sins? Jesus paid the debt for your sin, so there's no need for you to do anything. Are you hoping to win God's favor? You cannot be good enough for that; besides, those in Christ have received all the favor due a son!

The Lord doesn't expect us to barter for His favor. His love isn't for sale.

If, on the other hand, you desire to honor the Lord because you love Him, Micah offers an uncomplicated approach. God looks beneath and beyond all outward expressions of religious devotion to examine our character. What honors the Lord is a heart that beats in the same rhythm as His, a spirit that values the same qualities that define Him. He wants people who do what is right, who love kindness, and who walk humbly with Him. Do as Micah instructs, and you will not only honor the Lord you love, you will live life well.

GOD EXPECTS US TO DO WHAT IS RIGHT

"Do what is right." In this postmodern era, that statement requires clarification before we can proceed. Postmodernism has so blurred the line between right and wrong that young people have a difficult time discerning what kind of behavior is good, appropriate, and expected; what behavior is fundamentally wrong; and which choices are morally neutral. Most adults shy away from declaring their beliefs as hard and fast rules of conduct. Thanks to the postmodern worldview, it's considered foolish to declare that truth exists and boorish to suggest that one can have it.

I can say with genuine certainty and with absolutely no arrogance, *I have a direct line to absolute truth.* I didn't uncover it. I didn't create it. I wasn't the first to see it or even recognize it. I merely accept God's Word as authentic revelation from the Author of truth. The sixty-six books of the Bible provide us with God's directives and principles. He took the time to have His Word written down and preserved through the centuries so that we may know Him and obey His will. The Bible reflects His character, and by reading it we may discover what values and choices give Him the most pleasure. Therefore, to do what is right is to conform one's life to the directives and principles found in the sixty-six books of the Bible.

Right conduct cannot be determined by polling the opinion of others. Cultural unanimity will never guide us toward moral truth. We cannot trust our feelings to validate our choices—they are notoriously fickle. And we cannot assume that the easy path is one we should trust. In fact, choosing to do what is right will likely lead to misunderstanding or misrepresentation. Others may resent the trouble you cause when you refuse to support wrongdoing.

It could even put you on the wrong side of the law and invite persecution.

THE COST OF OBEDIENCE

Roughly 750 years after Micah's prophecy, two of Jesus' disciples wrestled with a deadly dilemma. After Jesus was crucified, buried, resurrected, and had ascended to heaven, His followers began to share the good news with everyone they met. And to prove the truth of their message, Peter and John healed a man who was paralyzed from birth, the same kind of miracle Jesus had performed numerous times before. But, despite this irrefutable proof, Israel's religious officials were determined to silence the message of salvation through Christ and destroy anyone who preached it.

> As they were speaking to the people, the priests and the captain of the temple guard and the Sadducees came up to them, being greatly disturbed because they were teaching the people and proclaiming in Jesus the resurrection

from the dead. And they laid hands on them and put them in jail until the next day, for it was already evening. But many of those who had heard the message believed; and the number of the men came to be about five thousand. (Acts 4:1–4)

In the first century, Sadducees were a political Jewish sect whose members believed that Israel's best policy was to appease Rome. Naturally, they tended to be wealthy and politically powerful. And because religious zealots might find a champion in a man calling himself "King of the Jews," they feared the widespread popularity of Jesus. They were certain that killing Him would keep the people disorganized and keep Rome's armies at home. So reports of a resurrected Jesus not only upset the balance again, they also gave the Sadducees an enemy they couldn't kill.

At first they claimed that someone had stolen the body of Jesus, but the rumor wouldn't take. Too many saw Him alive and well. And many more accepted the truth of His resurrection, which left the frantic Sadducees only one recourse: silence the witnesses. First, they tried intimidation.

On the next day, their rulers and elders and scribes were gathered together in Jerusalem; and Annas the high priest was there, and Caiaphas and John and Alexander, and all who were of high-priestly descent. When they had placed them in the center, they began to inquire, "By what power, or in what name, have you done this?" (Acts 4:5–7)

To appreciate the pressure Peter and John faced, imagine two American, high school educated, working-class, regular Joes hauled before a joint session of Congress and the Supreme Court without the benefit of legal representation. Standing in the foreboding presence of such intelligence and political power, the two simple fishermen heard the following demands: make a legal case for the actions you have taken. Explain why we shouldn't hand you over to the Romans and let them nail you to a cross.

The question, "By what power, or in what name, have you done this?" refers to their proclaiming the resurrection of Jesus. This wasn't a genuine question; it was a charge. The Sadducees already knew the answer. Peter knew this and courageously chose to preface his answer with a charge of his own.

> Then Peter, filled with the Holy Spirit, said to them, "Rulers and elders of the people, if we are on trial today for a benefit done to a sick man, as to how this man has been made well, let it be known to all of you and to all the people of Israel, that by the name of Jesus Christ the Nazarene, whom you crucified, whom God raised from the dead—by this name this man stands here before you in good health. [Jesus] is the stone which was rejected by you, the builders, but which became the chief corner stone. And there is salvation in no one else; for there is no other name under heaven that has been given among men by which we must be saved." (Acts 4:8–12)

Note two phrases in particular: "filled with the Holy Spirit" and "whom you crucified." To be filled with the Holy Spirit means to be controlled by the Spirit of God. And when you are under the full control of the Holy Spirit, immoral choices are impossible. In fact, when you submit yourself to the dominating control of the Holy Spirit, you are transformed from within, empowered to think clearly and act confidently. Peter boldly and shrewdly turned the Sadducees' accusation of insurrection around to show that they—not he and John—were the treasonous ones. His cryptic reference to "the stone which was rejected" points back to Jesus' words when these same men had brought the same charge against the Lord.

> When [Jesus] entered the temple, the chief priests and the elders of the people came to Him while He was teaching, and said, "By what authority are You doing these things, and who gave You this authority?" (Matthew 21:23)

In His reply to the chief priests (Sadducees) and the Pharisees, Jesus drew upon a metaphor in Psalm 118:22 to declare Himself to be Israel's Messiah, the nation's true King. Any Jew who was familiar with the Scriptures understood the claim with perfect clarity. The Messiah was to be the chief stone in the building called "the

Kingdom of God." Nevertheless, they plotted to kill their king and, in so doing, subverted the rightful government of their country.

So there stood Peter and John before the most powerful men in Israel, using this earlier memory to turn the accusation around. But in case anyone wasn't paying attention, Peter made his countercharge crystal clear. He said, in effect, "The King you killed is alive again, He is God, and you must come to Him—and no other—for salvation."

Can you hear the stunned silence that followed Peter's speech? These high-powered, religious authorities did their best to intimidate the two apostles into silence. But observe their response.

Now as [the rulers, elders, scribes, Annas, Caiaphas, John, Alexander, and all who were of high priestly ancestry] observed the confidence of Peter and John and understood that they were uneducated and untrained men, they were amazed, and began to recognize them as having been with Jesus. And seeing the man who had been healed standing with them, they had nothing to say in reply. (Acts 4:13–14)

Careful observation of this passage reveals no less than three qualities that distinguish a godly person when he or she chooses to do what is right. And each quality points to a principle we can apply to help us behave more like these two steadfast men.

First, observe the *confidence* of Peter and John. This is not arrogance. An arrogant person cannot walk humbly with God. The two men spoke with confidence because they found security in the Lord, not themselves.

Second, consider the *authority* of Peter and John. They were not formally trained in higher education to debate theology and philosophy as the Sadducees were. The apostles stood on Christ's authority, not their own. They possessed a direct line to absolute truth: Jesus Christ, the Living Word of God.

Third, see the *effectiveness* of Peter and John. Doing what is right—conforming one's conduct to the principles of Scripture and submitting to the control of the Holy Spirit—produces results. The undeniable effect of the apostles' obedience stood beside them: a formerly paralyzed man brought to perfect health.

Peter and John exemplify the first quality of a life well lived according to Micah 6:8. The quality of justice is the consistent, unwavering decision to do what is right. And when you choose to do what is right, you can walk and speak with complete confidence. Your thoughts and actions proceed from a clear understanding of truth. Though perhaps misunderstood, maligned, or even persecuted, you can walk with steadfast peace, knowing that the Lord understands, approves, and rewards those who remain faithful.

THE RESULT OF OBEDIENCE

Beyond any doubt, the religious officials were not ignorant. They knew that the apostles spoke the truth and that it was from God.

> But when they had ordered them to leave the Council, they began to confer with one another, saying, "What shall we do with these men? For the fact that a noteworthy miracle has taken place through them is apparent to all who live in Jerusalem, and we cannot deny it. But so

that it will not spread any further among the people, let us warn them to speak no longer to any man in this name." And when they had summoned them, they commanded [Peter and John] not to speak or teach at all in the name of Jesus. (Acts 4:15–18)

The two "uneducated and untrained men" could have remained quiet, taken their tongue lashing, left the council chambers, and carried on with their preaching ministry. Instead, they took issue with the unjust gag order and openly announced their intention to ignore it. But notice, there is no hint of haughtiness or insolence in their speech. Just the humble declaration of two simple fishermen who had news too good to keep quiet, a truth too big to hide.

"Whether it is right in the sight of God to give heed to you rather than to God, you be the judge; for we cannot stop speaking about what we have seen and heard." When [the counsel] had threatened them further, they let [John and Peter] go (finding no basis on which to punish them) on account of the people, because they were all glorifying God for what had happened; for the man was more than forty years old on whom this miracle of healing had been performed. (Acts 4:19–22)

Peter and John knew what was right. Their respect for the religious leaders didn't blind them to their duty before the Lord. Jesus had said, "Go . . . make disciples . . . teaching them to observe all that I commanded you" (Matthew 28:19–20), and "You shall be My witnesses" (Acts 1:8). This gave them the courage to obey God rather than people. And, in this case, their enemies had no choice but to honor their dedication. Peter and John's followers— the rest of the disciples and the thousands of believers who had proclaimed the resurrection of Jesus Christ— shouted and sang and prayed in celebration.

And when they had prayed, the place where they had gathered together was shaken, and they were all filled with the Holy Spirit and began to speak the word of God with boldness. (Acts 4:31)

The obedience Peter and John sowed that day returned an abundant harvest. Obedience encouraged more obedience. And "abundant grace was upon them all" (Acts 4:33).

At this point, I would love to end with the fairytale words "and they preached happily ever after." But, as is usually the case in this fallen world of ours, no good deed shall go unpunished. As obedience—doing what is right—grows, opposition will develop in direct proportion. The news of Peter and John's earlier healing of the paralyzed man spread, which brought multitudes to Jerusalem, hoping to have the miracle repeated. And, before long, the apostles found themselves facing an increasingly agitated body of religious leaders.

And all the more believers in the Lord, multitudes of men and women, were constantly added to their number, to such an extent that they even carried the sick out into the streets and laid them on cots and pallets, so that when Peter came by at least his shadow might fall on any one of them. Also the people from the cities in the vicinity of Jerusalem were coming together, bringing people who were sick or afflicted with unclean spirits, and they were all being healed.

But the high priest rose up, along with all his associates

(that is the sect of the Sadducees), and they were filled with jealousy. They laid hands on the apostles and put them in a public jail. (Acts 5:14–18)

The foolish, two-dimensional thinking of the religious elite led them to believe that the followers of Jesus would respond to coercion, that they would be discouraged by the loss of personal freedom and creature comforts. But Peter and John's ethics extended beyond the approval of people and above the earthly plane to include the vertical dimension. They were miraculously released from prison, and instead of fleeing the city, they returned to the temple to resume their proclamation of Christ's resurrection. When they were again brought before the religious council and challenged to stop their preaching, the apostles responded with words we would all do well to memorize:

> "WE MUST OBEY GOD RATHER THAN MEN." (ACTS 5:29)

The leaders of Israel were almost resolved to dispose of the believers as they had done to Jesus. But a highly respected teacher named Gamaliel made an astute observation concerning the result of obedience.

If this plan or action is of men, it will be overthrown; but if it is of God, you will not be able to overthrow them; or else you may even be found fighting against God. (Acts 5:38–39)

To do what is right is to side with the truth of God. And never doubt it, the truth of God will always prevail. Evil may cause setbacks and it may hamper the steady march of God's plan, but it is ultimately powerless to stop it. To do what is right is to join the winning side of the fight, though the battle will not be without pain or struggle.

The men of the council took the advice of Gamaliel, the respected teacher, and released the apostles. But they couldn't deny their bloodlust. Before letting the followers of Jesus go free, they subjected them to the same kind of scourging their Master endured. If you saw the film *The*

Passion of The Christ, you saw an accurate portrayal of this brutal Roman punishment. Victims were beaten within an inch of their lives and very often died from their wounds. Recovery could take months. Nevertheless . . .

> They went on their way from the presence of the Council, rejoicing that they had been considered worthy to suffer shame for His name. And every day, in the temple and from house to house, they kept right on teaching and preaching Jesus as the Christ. (Acts 5:41–42)

Meaning? They kept doing what was right!

Doing What Is Right
in the Twenty-First Century

A quick review of history reveals the impact these faithful men had on the world. Within just a few generations, much of the Roman world had been saturated with the gospel. Less than two hundred years later Christianity became the official religion of the Empire. While, admittedly, that may not have been the best thing to happen to the church, it nonetheless demonstrates the powerful effect of people doing what is right.

The principles that applied more than two thousand years ago still apply today. The effect of doing what is right is no less powerful. But more important, it's what the Lord expects of those who call themselves Christian. He has a plan, and He calls us to become a part of it. Three time-less, practical principles will help us do just that.

We must know what is right.

Obviously we cannot *do* what is right if we don't *know* what is right. Unfortunately our culture is awash with information and opinions and philosophies and ideolo-gies—all in the context of a postmodern worldview that doubts the very existence of definable truth.

I am also concerned by what I see as a growing trend in evangelical churches—the notion that God reveals truth directly to our hearts in spoken and unspoken messages, that we can receive truth or directives or instructions from the Lord. I often hear people say things like, "I wasn't sure what to do about that job offer until the Lord spoke to my heart and told me what to do," or "I haven't made a decision yet; I'm waiting to hear from God on that."

Let me be clear. In the past, the Lord spoke to people directly—via visual and audible manifestations of Himself, in dreams and visions, even in silence—and His purpose was to have them convey those supernaturally communicated messages to others or write them down for future generations. We have a record of those messages preserved in the sixty-six books of the Bible. Once the Bible was complete, the Lord stopped supernaturally speaking to people directly. He then replaced this method with one much greater, one much more intimate.

In the old covenant, God issued orders that He expected to be fulfilled to the letter. But in the new covenant, He has stopped issuing orders. Instead, He sent His Holy Spirit to transform the heart of the believer, to renew his or her mind to think as the Father thinks. He no longer shouts to the faithful, in effect, "Drop and give Me twenty pushups!" Now He reforms the character of His people so that they will say within, "I want to give You fifty!" In a process called *sanctification*, God transforms the character of the believer to match that of His Son, creating agents who think like He thinks, behave as He desires, and make choices that reflect His values and accomplish His will.

Therefore, as you seek to do what is right, don't look for God's voice within saying, "Turn left. Take this job, not that one. Read your Bible. Eat less fat." Instead, make use of the resources God has made available to you. Let me mention just three.

1. *Let God reveal to you what is right from His Word.* Read your Bible, not to discover what hurdles you must clear or what hoops you need to jump through in order to make the Lord happy, but to become increasingly intimate with His character. Set aside the newspapers and magazines, turn off the television, cancel some appointments, and make time to get into God's inspired, reliable Word. Discover timeless facts and principles directly from the Author of truth. Allow the reading of Scripture to prompt new perspectives and trigger new insights.

2. *Trust the transforming power of the Holy Spirit to lead you toward what is right.* As the Holy Spirit does His work of gradual transformation, listen to your inner convictions. They are not the voice of God. They are the thoughts of a mind changed to think like the Lord Himself. Your old character and values will be exchanged for the Lord's so that you begin to think with the mind of Christ. This is far better than some people's idea of the new covenant in which God merely barks orders from inside the heart rather than through a prophet or in writing.

3. *Heed the wisdom of those who follow Christ and who do what is right.* God gave us His Word, He gave us His Spirit, and He gave us one another. Paul the apostle wrote, "Be imitators of me, just as I also am of Christ" (1 Corinthians 11:1), and "Now you followed my teaching, conduct, purpose, faith, patience, love, perseverance, persecutions, and sufferings" (2 Timothy 3:10–11). I urge you to find a seasoned follower of Jesus and let his or her experience become a guide for your own journey.

We must expect resistance.

When we choose to do what is right and meet with resistance, a common reaction is to wonder, *Where did I go wrong? Did I displease God?* The answer is, quite simply, no. The bold choice to do something that honors the Lord or reflects His character will be punished by a world that is opposed to His way. Peter and John received a flogging for their faithfulness, a punishment normally reserved for criminals.

You may lose popularity. You might be denied opportunities you rightfully deserve. You might be persecuted for taking a stand for truth, or for defending the innocent, or for refusing to look the other way while others do wrong. Don't expect to be rewarded. Expect resistance. That doesn't mean you should become discouraged or timid, but don't be surprised when (not if) you face difficulties as a result of doing what is right.

We must remember that God will superintend His plan.

Walking the path that the prophet Micah marked for us will never be easy. When the going gets tough, remind yourself that you are not alone. It would have been easy for

Peter and John, sitting in their jail cells, to wonder if the Lord had forgotten them. They were faithful to proclaim the message they had been given, they were busy carrying out Jesus' commission to make disciples, and jail time was the thanks they received. But instead of becoming bitter, they rejoiced!

What kept them hopeful despite the imprisonment and the floggings was the trust they had placed in the Lord. He warned that they would drink of the same cup that He was to drink, but that ultimate victory was certain. His resurrection secured the eventual triumph of His kingdom, which gave the apostles courage to stand strong in the face of severe persecution. They knew God was in control. That meant they were fighting for the winning side. It is remarkable how invincible such knowledge can make you feel.

When you find yourself being punished for doing what is right, you have joined the ranks of a very distinguished league. You and I have a great "cloud of witnesses surrounding us" (Hebrews 12:1). We are following in the steps of faithful men and women who extended the kingdom of God and made the world a better place, and did so at great personal cost. Fearlessly do as they did. Trust that God is right in all His ways, and take courage in the fact that you, too, fight for the winning side. As David once wrote, "Through God we shall do valiantly" (Psalm 60:12).

Chapter 2

Loving What's Kind

Ours is an age in which the most coveted commodity is not gold but time. All too quickly we forego the opportunity to be kind in order to gain a few extra minutes. And we typically don't even realize that we've made that exchange. I can tell you from my own experience it's a poor trade. I know that whenever I begin to treat people as obstacles in my path or use them as merely a means to getting things done, I become a smaller man. With each brusque comment, each dismissive glance, each curt reply, I lose a little more of myself. To make matters worse, my relationship with God suffers.

When you and I find ourselves exchanging kindness for a few extra minutes, we're too busy. This is not the only reason for lack of kindness, but it's certainly one of the most common.

Rediscover Kindness

Merriam-Webster's Collegiate Dictionary defines *kind* as "of a sympathetic or helpful nature, of a forbearing nature, gentle."[1] Let's face it. None of that flows naturally. Kindness takes time, yet we're usually in a rush. Kindness requires us to empathize with others, yet we are by nature self-centered. Kindness calls for compassion, yet judgment typically comes more naturally. Kindness demands a forgiving attitude, yet we find revenge more appealing. Nevertheless, kindness is what the Lord expects of us. My good friend and colleague at Dallas Theological Seminary, Dr. Jeff Bingham, once said, "You can't truly love God and not love the people He made."

In answering the question, what does the Lord expect of us? Micah states that we are to "love kindness." In doing so, he points to the rich Hebrew term *chesed* (the *ch* is pronounced with a hard, guttural 'k' sound). That colorful word is so steeped in Hebrew culture and theology that it has no equivalent in other languages. That explains why *chesed* has been rendered by different translations as "mercy," "kindness," "loving-kindness," "goodness," and others. It describes God's covenant love for His people—a passionate, merciful, pursuing, unrelenting kindness that overlooks their inability to repay Him or even return His love.

The Bible is filled with wonderful, moving stories that show *chesed* in action. When Ruth and her mother-in-law, Naomi, became widows, Ruth declared, "Do not urge me to leave you or turn back from following you; for where you go, I will go, and where you lodge, I will lodge. Your people shall be my people, and your God, my God. Where you die, I will die, and there I will be buried" (Ruth 1:16–17). She demonstrated extraordinary kindness in her devotion to her mother-in-law.

Jonathan, the son of King Saul, extended extraordinary kindness to David. Even as his own father sought to kill David, Jonathan remained steadfastly loyal to his friend. His loyalty cost him favor with Saul, as well as any hope of becoming king of Israel. Nevertheless, "Jonathan loved him as himself" (1 Samuel 18:1).

When David eventually became king, he extended

extraordinary kindness to Mephibosheth, the son of Jonathan. In that day, the first official act of a new king was to execute everyone associated with the old dynasty for fear of future rebellion. Even a distant cousin in the old family might attract enough dissenters to cause trouble. But David went out of his way to find and bless the young man. When Saul's grandson stood trembling before David, the king said, "Do not fear, for I will surely show kindness to you for the sake of your father Jonathan, and will restore to you all the land of your grandfather Saul; and you shall eat at my table regularly" (2 Samuel 9:7).

A woman living in Shunem noticed the prophet Elisha passed her house often in his travels, so she said to her husband, "I perceive that this is a holy man of God passing by us continually. Please, let us make a little walled upper chamber and let us set a bed for him there, and a table and a chair and a lampstand; and it shall be, when he comes to us, that he can turn in there" (2 Kings 4:9–10). This was no small act of kindness, and it was a great help in the ministry of Elisha.

Of course, we have no greater example of kindness than God Himself. And no expression of that kindness is better demonstrated than His becoming a human in the person of Jesus Christ. The Gospel accounts show Jesus extending kindness to others throughout His earthly ministry. Furthermore, when Paul listed the qualities of the quintessential Christian life, he concluded with the words, "Be kind to one another, tender-hearted, forgiving each other, just as God in Christ also has forgiven you" (Ephesians 4:32). The Greek word is *chrestos*, which means "useful, good of its kind, serviceable."[2] The word sounds a lot like *christos*, the Greek rendering of the title "Christ." How appropriate that the two words should sound so much alike. To be kind is to be like Christ. A kind heart freely forgives just as Christ forgave.

THE GREATEST CHALLENGE TO KINDNESS

Perhaps the greatest challenge to kindness is an injury caused by another. If we can focus our efforts on mastering the art of forgiveness, I believe other acts of kindness will naturally follow. Genesis 45 tells a story of extraordinary kindness. It depicts a monumental act of forgiveness that will challenge us, inspire us, and give us an unforgettable example of what it means to forgive.

The story begins in Genesis 37 with a naïve, seventeen-year-old son of a wealthy Hebrew living in ancient Canaan. Joseph's father doted on him, and Joseph made no secret of the fact that he was loved more than his ten older brothers, which gave them plenty of reason to despise him. Eventually their growing hatred turned to violence as they plotted to kill their brother and dump his body in a cistern out in the wilderness. Fortunately, the restraint of the eldest brother convinced the others to sell him into slavery instead. After a quick-n-dirty transaction with a caravan of traders, he was on his way to Egypt in chains. To cover their crime, Joseph's brothers smeared his multicolored tunic—a special gift from his father—with goat's blood and convinced their dad that an animal had killed the boy.

Put yourself in Joseph's place. You're a high school senior, quietly living your life in relative comfort and contemplating a bright future. Then, a thump on the head, the world goes black, and you wake up miles from home, chained to the bed of a pickup truck, headed who knows where. After several days of travel, you arrive in a foreign land. You're dragged by your chains onto a small platform as a crowd presses in to poke and gawk at you. The strangers speak a language you don't know, but nevertheless you understand what's happening. They're bidding . . . for you.

The young man's life as he knew it was over. The favored son had become a foreign slave—and in Egypt of all places!

Joseph became the property of Potiphar, Pharaoh's chief bodyguard, in whose house he learned the language and culture of the Egyptians. In the course of time, he proved himself both wise and faithful in the management of the tasks assigned to him and eventually became the chief steward. It's not hard to imagine that Joseph thought of home continually and perhaps believed he might win the favor of his master, maybe even his freedom. But an unfortunate twist of circumstances dashed his hopes.

Potiphar's wife had made multiple sexual advances toward Joseph. Each time he tactfully but firmly rejected her proposition. After a final, bold attempt to seduce him, she resented his rejection and accused him of attempted rape, a charge that her husband took at face value. The word of the woman of the house against that of a slave made for a speedy conviction, and as quickly as he had become a slave, he became an inmate. Imagine how he must have felt about his treacherous brothers those first hours in that dark and dangerous Egyptian dungeon. All of this was their fault, yet we read nothing of Joseph's becoming bitter.

Despite his kindness to the other inmates and his trustworthiness before the guards, he languished in prison for more than two years. Even those who committed to helping him get out soon forgot their promises. Eventually, though, the Lord used an array of circumstances not only to free Joseph but to install him as Pharaoh's prime minister. As second in command, it was his job to see this superpower of the ancient world through a seven-year famine.

In a matter of a few days, Joseph went from prisoner-slave to prime minister. And as one of the most powerful men in Egypt, he almost certainly outranked Potiphar. Yet we find no indication that he went back for revenge.

Meanwhile, "back on the ranch" in Canaan, Joseph's father and brothers struggled to survive the famine. Unable to grow crops of their own, they were forced to travel to Egypt in the hope of purchasing food. Genesis 42–45 describes Joseph's reunion with his brothers, when they appeared before him to ask for help. Of course, they had no idea that the top-ranked official of the Egyptian government was, in fact, the very brother they had sold into slavery more than twelve years earlier. He looked different, he spoke through an interpreter, and he wore the official garb of the Egyptian high command. After a series of interviews and tests of their character, Joseph could contain himself no longer. Try to imagine the following scene.

Then Joseph could not control himself before all those who stood by him, and he cried, "Have everyone go out from me." So there was no man with him when Joseph made himself known to his brothers. He wept so loudly that the Egyptians heard it, and the household of Pharaoh heard of it. Then Joseph said to his brothers, "I am Joseph! Is my father still alive?" But his brothers could not answer him, for they were dismayed at his presence. Then Joseph said to his brothers, "Please come closer to me." And they came closer. And he said, "I am your brother Joseph, whom you sold into Egypt." (Genesis 45:1–4)

The Hebrew word rendered "dismayed" usually describes someone trembling with terror. Joseph's brothers had every reason to fear. And—let's be honest—Joseph had every reason to use the power of his position to give his brothers a "thumbs down," resulting in ten times the torment he had suffered. But take note of the kindness of his character.

Now do not be grieved or angry with yourselves, because you sold me here, for God sent me before you to preserve life. For the famine has been in the land these two years, and there are still five years in which there will be neither plowing nor harvesting. God sent me before you to preserve for you a remnant in the earth, and to keep you alive by a great deliverance. Now, therefore, it was not you who sent me here, but God; and He has made me a father to Pharaoh and lord of all his household and ruler over all the land of Egypt. Hurry and go up to my father, and say to him, "Thus says your son Joseph, 'God has made me lord of all Egypt; come down to me, do not delay.'" (Genesis 45:5–9)

Observe that there are no accusations or judgments against his treacherous brothers. Instead of "you, you, you, you, you . . . ," there are no less than five divine attributions giving credit to God for His wise foresight and sovereignty. Then Joseph used the power of his position to heap blessing upon mercy.

"You shall live in the land of Goshen, and you shall be near me, you and your children and your children's children and your flocks and your herds and all that you have. There I will also provide for you, for there are still five years of famine to come, and you and your household and all that you have would be impoverished."

He kissed all his brothers and wept on them, and afterward his brothers talked with him. (Genesis 45:10–11, 15)

Joseph remained true to his word. The brothers traveled to Canaan and returned to Egypt with their father and everything they owned. They settled in a region of Egypt called Goshen and enjoyed Joseph's protection and provision over the next seventeen years, until their father died. Then the brothers began to wonder again. Was Joseph kind to them on account of their father? Had he merely postponed judgment against them? Rather than leave the matter to chance, the brothers concocted a story and sent a message to Joseph:

Your father charged before he died, saying, "Thus you shall say to Joseph, 'Please forgive, I beg you, the transgression of your brothers and their sin, for they did you wrong.'" And now, please forgive the transgression of the servants of the God of your father. (Genesis 50:16–17)

How sad that they didn't take the time to discover Joseph's character. They had nearly two decades after their reunion to spend time with him and learn from his experiences. I imagine that's why Joseph wept upon hearing their message and then summoned them for a meeting. He had consistently demonstrated a forgiving attitude and had treated them with kindness. Yet all of his attempts to reach out and establish a relationship were met with fear and suspicion. How lonely this must have made him feel!

And Joseph wept when they spoke to him. Then his brothers also came and fell down before him and said, "Behold, we are your servants." But Joseph said to them, "Do not be afraid, for am I in God's place? As for you, *you meant evil against me, but God meant it for good* in order to bring about this present result, to preserve many people alive. So therefore, do not be afraid; I will provide for you and your little ones." So he comforted them and spoke kindly to them. (Genesis 50:17–21, italics mine)

Joseph personified extraordinary kindness.

The Hebrew behind the phrase "spoke kindly to them" is literally translated "spoke to their hearts." It's an idiom that means Joseph shaped his reassurances to address their deepest concerns. He not only knew their deepest concerns, he cared enough to ease them without chastisement or judgment.

My son, do not forget my teaching,
*   But let your heart keep my commandments;*
For length of days and years of life
*   And peace they will add to you.*
Do not let kindness and truth leave you;
*   Bind them around your neck,*
*   Write them on the tablet of your heart.*
So you will find favor and good repute
*   In the sight of God and man.*

—PROVERBS 3:1–4

What a kind man we find in Joseph! Despite a lifetime of cruel and unfair treatment, injustice, and misunderstanding—a life in which he was nearly always punished for doing what was right—he never became resentful. He never drank the toxic combination of bitterness and revenge, that poisonous concoction that not only destroys the lives of others but corrodes the vessel that contains it. Joseph refused to harbor either, which left him free to "love kindness."

THE WAY OF KINDNESS

Cultivating a kind heart is a challenge for any generation. Whether in ancient Egypt or high-tech America, the depravity of humankind will give us plenty of reasons to adopt a condemning, pharisaical attitude. Others will always deserve our criticism, for they will never fail to disappoint. Nevertheless, the Lord expects us to love *chrestos*, kindness. Brennan Manning refers to this quality as "tenderness" in his insightful book *Abba's Child*:

The betrayals and infidelities in my life are too numerous to count. I still cling to the illusion that I must be morally impeccable, other people must be sinless, and the one I love must be without human weakness. But whenever I allow anything but tenderness and compassion to dictate my response to life—be it self-righteous anger, moralizing, defensiveness, the pressing need to change others, carping criticism, frustration at others' blindness, a sense of spiritual superiority, a gnawing hunger of vindication—I am alienated from my true self. My identity as Abba's child becomes ambiguous, tentative, and confused.

Our way of being in the world is the way of tenderness. Everything else is illusion, misperception, falsehood.

The compassionate way of life is neither a sloppy goodwill toward the world nor the plague of what Robert Wicks calls "chronic niceness." It does not insist that a widow become friendly with her husband's murderer. It does not demand that we like everyone. It does not wink at sin and injustice. . . .

The way of tenderness avoids blind fanaticism. Instead,

it seeks to see with penetrating clarity. The compassion of God in our hearts opens our eyes to the unique worth of each person. "The other is 'ourself'; and we must love him in his sin as we were loved in our sin."[3]

I find three principles at work in the life of Joseph that I believe will help us choose the way of kindness as we face our own injustices, both small and great. These are truths that I find helpful when I notice that carping criticism and self-righteous anger have displaced kindness in me.

Let God be the Judge.

When I realize I'm not "in God's place," the desire for revenge fades. By that I mean that I do not presume to become God in someone else's life. It's the Holy Spirit's responsibility to convict of sin, to produce spiritual maturity, to make a person better. I do not presume to be his or her Christ. He has sovereign control; He is that person's king, not me. Only He has the right to sit in judgment over the flawed character of another. He earned that right by atoning for sin and offering redemption, something I can never do.

As I recuse myself from the judge's bench and allow God to dispense justice and mercy at His pleasure, I feel less desire to handle them myself.

Let God be the Manager.

When I acknowledge God's sovereign hand in all circumstances, I am better able to tolerate the injustices of the world. The unjust suffering I have endured pales in comparison to the trials Joseph faced. Yet he was able to reflect upon the events of his life and say, "You meant evil against me, but God meant it for good" (Genesis 50:20).

Many of our difficulties will come as a result of the sin or failure of others, yet we cannot deny that God allowed them. While we suffer the consequences of choices we did not make, the Lord is nonetheless in complete control of our lives. He never promised to shield us from harm, but we have His assurance that everything we experience will be used to shape our character and prepare us for future blessing (Romans 8:28).

(I suggest you read that paragraph again, more slowly.)

As I yield control of my life to God, accepting that every circumstance is from His hand, I find that I'm unable to resent others. Bitterness cannot take root in any soul where resentment has not prepared the soil.

Let your heart be free.

When I am truly free of the desire for revenge and have accepted my circumstances as God's means of blessing, I find room in my heart for kindness. The human heart is like a vessel, and because it has limited space, I have to be careful what I choose to carry in it. Furthermore, whatever I choose to carry is all I have to give. If I let it fill up with the bitter gall of resentment, my loved ones, colleagues, and parishioners will not have priority in my life. Instead, my thoughts will center on myself, and my energy will be spent on the futile pursuit of fairness.

However, as I allow God to be the God of others and place all circumstances under His sovereignty, I have created space for grace. And as grace is absorbed in my life, kindness begins to flow naturally and freely.

A Word to Husbands and Fathers

I have observed that men tend to resist kindness more than women do. And so my closing words in this section are deliberately directed to my fellow husbands and fathers. We can be so focused on doing what is right, providing for the family, solving problems, and preparing for the future that we overlook something very important to our wives and children. Few things impact them more positively than random acts of kindness by you: a tangible expression of love, choosing to *under*react to a petty offense or failure, an unexpected affirmation, setting aside work for a few uninterrupted moments. These are the things memories are made of. These are what people, especially those in your family, will remember when you are gone—not your provision, not the tasks you faithfully completed, not the problems you solved. That may seem unfair, but trust me on this: those who are closest to you will remember your kindness first and foremost.

Ken Gire wrote the following words in his fine volume *A Father's Gift: The Legacy of Memories*. I find them very sobering and convicting as I consider my own role as husband, father, and grandfather.

What pictures will *my* son remember
    when he comes to the plain granite marker
    over *his* father's grave?
    What will my daughters remember?
    Or my wife?
What pictures will be left behind
    for them to thumb through
    in the nostalgic, late afternoons
    of their lives?
Will the pictures strengthen them for the journey?
    Or send them hobbling through life, crippled. . . .
I've resolved to give fewer lectures,
    to send fewer platitudes rolling their way,
    to give less criticism,
    to offer fewer opinions.
After all, where does it say that a father
    has to voice an opinion on everything?
    Or even *have* an opinion on everything?

From now on, I'll give them pictures they can live by,
  pictures that can comfort them,
  encourage them,
  and keep them warm
  in my absence.
Because when I'm gone, there will only be silence.
  And memories. . . .
Of all
  I could give
  to make their lives a little fuller,
  a little richer,
  a little more prepared
  for the journey ahead of them,
  nothing compares to the gift of remembrance—
  pictures that show they are special
  and that they are loved.
Pictures that will be there
  when I am not.
Pictures that have within them
  a redemption all their own.[4]

On a recent trip to Israel with a large group, my wife and I were making our way down the Mount of Olives when we came to a little plateau overlooking an old grave-yard. The stones were dark with age, and many of the epi-taphs were barely legible. One of our number asked the Hebrew-speaking guide to read some of the gravestones, most of which read simply, "In honor of . . ." After reading a few at random, she came to the epitaph of a holocaust survivor, a man who had endured the horrors of Auschwitz and finally settled in Israel. The etchings on the man's gravestone ended with these words: "He pursued *chesed*."

What do you want yours to say?

Chapter 3

Modeling What's Humble

WHEN I READ JESS MOODY'S DESCRIPTION OF HIS uncle Zeke in the book *A Drink at Joel's Place*, I wondered if he had mistaken one of my distant relatives for his. But then I think we all know at least one Uncle Zeke.

One day the village blacksmith was hammering a glowing red horseshoe. He happened to hit it a little awry and it fell into the dust near the door.

Just about that time, Uncle Zeke came in and saw the horseshoe which had just lost its reddened glow, but was still hot as a depot stove.

Zeke reached down and picked up the horseshoe. Of course, he immediately threw it down.

"What's the matter, Zeke, is it hot?" laughed a group of onlookers.

Zeke raised his pride-filled self to his highest height and answered, "No, it just don't take me long to look at a horseshoe."[5]

Within each one of us a battle rages between the ugly sin of pride and the rare virtue of humility, the desire for status versus the longing for Christlikeness. It's a war we like to keep private. We rarely acknowledge it, we are reluctant to reveal it, and we secretly wonder if our own heart is the only one torn by this great conflict. Let me assure you, every heart is a battlefield. The fighting only subsides when the heart stops beating.

The only person who was able to defeat the enemy of pride was the Son of God, who modestly revealed, "I am gentle and humble in heart" (Matthew 11:29). He sandwiched this bit of self-revelation between an invitation and a promise. He invited everyone, "Come to Me.... Take My yoke upon you and learn from Me." And He promised, "You will find rest for your souls" (Matthew 11:28–29).

This invitation to walk with God is an invitation to humility. It's an invitation to rest from the struggle to look like you've got it all together. It's an invitation to lay aside the burden of always having to be right. This is an invitation to be who you are—warts and all—without excuse, or apology, or feeling like you have to live up to someone's standard in order to be loved or respected. It's an invitation to cease the futile struggle to earn respectability and to enter God's rest.

Being Uncle Zeke is exhausting! Humility is so much easier, and so freeing.

Though we can never fully escape the inner conflict, we can find rest in the grace of God through His Son. I am comforted that the third expectation in Micah's letter does *not* read, "walk humbly," but "walk humbly *with your God*" (Micah 6:8, italics mine).

The Lord does not expect us to defeat the enemy of pride and master the virtue of humility. His expectation is that we would recognize our utter inability to conquer this foe on our own and to draw close to Him. He expects that we allow Him to teach us and that we submit our hearts to His process of transformation. I've learned that such transformation often involves being crushed.

> *"The devil, things and people being what they
> are, it is necessary for God to use the hammer,
> the file and the furnace in His holy work of
> preparing a saint for true sainthood. It is
> doubtful whether God can bless a man greatly
> until He has hurt him deeply."[6]*
>
> — A. W. Tozer

We learned from the example of Peter and John what it means to do what is right. We allowed the example of Joseph to show us kindness. Now, the life of the once mighty King David will highlight the many facets of the rare gem called humility.

HUMILITY DOESN'T KEEP SCORE

The story of David begins with an obscure, underestimated young man tending sheep in the Judean wilderness. As the youngest of eight sons, he was summoned only as an afterthought when Samuel came to the house of Jesse to find and anoint Israel's next king. In a few moments, oil ran down David's neck, and in an instant, the Spirit of God left Saul and rested on David.

"You younger men, likewise, be subject to your elders; and all of you, clothe yourselves with humility toward one another, for God is opposed to the proud, but gives grace to the humble. Therefore humble yourselves under the mighty hand of God, that He may exalt you at the proper time, casting all your anxiety on Him, because He cares for you."

— 1 PETER 5:5–7

Though he was anointed to be the true king of Israel, it would be almost two decades before he would actually sit on the throne. Soon after his anointing, the new king was back among his bleating companions on a hillside outside

Bethlehem. He didn't ride straight to Saul, swagger into the royal court, and demand his crown. The humble youth quietly returned to his household duties and waited for the Lord to exalt him at the proper time.

Before long, David was summoned to ease King Saul's foul mood with his singing and songwriting. Since his anointing, he had gained a reputation as "a skillful musician, a mighty man of valor, a warrior, one prudent in speech, and a handsome man." Of David, it was said, "the LORD is with him" (1 Samuel 16:18). Saul came to enjoy and admire David enough to make him his armor-bearer.

The irony is subtle, but profound. The rightful sovereign of the kingdom willingly became a personal valet to the man who was ill-qualified to occupy his throne. And when King David wasn't polishing Saul's armor, he was tending sheep in faithful service to his father.

Eventually the time ripened for David to begin his rise to power. A bellowing Philistine giant gave the Lord an opportunity to shine a spotlight on the future king. While Saul and the Israelite army cowered in their foxholes, David stood strong in his faith. Confident, yet humble, he performed valiantly on the field of battle and gave God the credit for the victory. In the weeks that followed, David's fame began to grow among the citizens of Israel. But as his popularity swelled, so did the pride of Saul. Soon, King Saul viewed him with suspicion. Envy turned to thoughts of murder. Within a few weeks, David had to flee into the wilderness, where he would live as a refugee for a dozen years or more while Saul and his army hunted him down.

During this very difficult and confusing time, David "strengthened himself in the LORD" (1 Samuel 30:6). He deliberately resisted the temptation to rush ahead of God's timing. Again and again, he displayed astounding patience. On one occasion, Saul led his army on an expedition to find and destroy David. While on the hunt, Saul entered a cave to relieve himself, not realizing that his rival sat in the shadows, blade drawn, only inches away. At that moment, David could have claimed what was rightfully his, and no one would have criticized him for doing what any natural man would have done. Nevertheless, he humbly restrained himself, choosing to wait on the Lord.

David's extraordinary character illustrates an important aspect of humility. Humility chooses to *receive* what is provided rather than *take* what is demanded. Humility never pulls rank, never gloats in victory, never demands its rights.

Humility Accepts Responsibility for Wrongdoing

Eventually David received the crown of Israel and quickly accomplished what Saul could only dream of doing. Within a few short seasons, all of Israel's local enemies were silenced by David's superior military strategy. He multiplied the kingdom's land tenfold, stabilized and expanded the economy, established secure trade routes, and proved himself an able statesman. On the spiritual front, he became the nation's lead worshiper, writing psalms, reviving the sacrifices, securing the ark of the covenant, gathering material to build a magnificent temple for the glory of God, and using the power of the throne to give the Lord first place among His chosen people.

"Then it happened." Those awful words open 2 Samuel 11, the darkest chapter in the life of David. When he normally would have been leading his troops on the field of battle, he delegated the job to his secretary of war, Joab. That wasn't wrong in itself, but the idleness gave temptation a greater opportunity to turn his head. He saw the wife of Uriah, his longtime friend, lusted after her, and then determined to sleep with her. The affair caused a royal scandal, which included an illegitimate pregnancy, a murder, and a cover-up.

After David spent several agonizing months in spiritual deadness, the prophet Nathan confronted the king with his sin. He cleverly baited David into judging himself with a story about a rich man who had taken a poor man's only, beloved lamb and served it for dinner to some important guests. Outraged, David demanded punishment for the rich man's cruelty. But when Nathan told David, "You are the man," he immediately responded, "I have sinned against the Lord" (2 Samuel 12). No denial. No explanations. No excuses. No bargaining or blame shifting. He didn't minimize the sin. He didn't blame the messenger. He didn't hide behind his office. And he certainly didn't try to make a distinction between his public and private life. David humbly accepted full responsibility for the wrong he had done. And the fruit of his humility is recorded in the moving words of Psalm 51. He dipped his stylus into a bowl of ink and, with a contrite heart, placed these words at the top of the page: "For the choir director. A Psalm of David, when Nathan the prophet came to him, after he had gone in to Bathsheba." What a triumph for grace! A broken man returns in humility to his God. As C. H. Spurgeon commented:

> When the divine message had aroused his dormant conscience and made him see the greatness of his guilt, he wrote this Psalm. He had forgotten his psalmody while he was indulging his flesh, but he returned to his harp when his spiritual nature was awakened, and he poured out his song to the accompaniment of sighs and tears. . . . He was a man of very strong passions, a soldier, and an Oriental monarch having despotic power; no other king of his time would have felt any compunction for having acted as he did, and hence there were not around him those restraints of custom

and association which, when broken through, render the offence the more monstrous. He never hints at any form of extenuation, nor do we mention these facts in order to apologize for his sin. . . . When we remember his sin, let us dwell most upon his penitence.[7]

Be gracious to me, O God, according to Your
lovingkindness;
According to the greatness of Your compassion blot out
my transgressions.
Wash me thoroughly from my iniquity
And cleanse me from my sin.
For I know my transgressions,
And my sin is ever before me.
Against You, You only, I have sinned
And done what is evil in Your sight,
So that You are justified when You speak
And blameless when You judge.
Behold, I was brought forth in iniquity,
And in sin my mother conceived me.

Behold, You desire truth in the innermost being,
    And in the hidden part You will make me know
    wisdom.
Purify me with hyssop, and I shall be clean;
    Wash me, and I shall be whiter than snow.
Make me to hear joy and gladness,
    Let the bones which You have broken rejoice.
Hide Your face from my sins
    And blot out all my iniquities.
Create in me a clean heart, O God,
    And renew a steadfast spirit within me.
Do not cast me away from Your presence
    And do not take Your Holy Spirit from me.
Restore to me the joy of Your salvation
    And sustain me with a willing spirit.
Then I will teach transgressors Your ways,
    And sinners will be converted to You.
Deliver me from bloodguiltiness, O God, the God of my
    salvation;
Then my tongue will joyfully sing of Your
    righteousness.

O Lord, open my lips,
  That my mouth may declare Your praise.
For You do not delight in sacrifice, otherwise I would
  give it;
You are not pleased with burnt offering.
  The sacrifices of God are a broken spirit;
A broken and a contrite heart, O God, You will not
  despise.
By Your favor do good to Zion;
  Build the walls of Jerusalem.
Then You will delight in righteous sacrifices,
  In burnt offering and whole burnt offering;
  Then young bulls will be offered on Your altar.

—Psalm 51

Psalm 51 is a prayer offered in complete humility by a broken man who was entirely aware of his fallen nature and the sin it can produce. In a word, David was crushed. In this prayer, Spurgeon finds four destructive traits that are absent from a heart that has been crushed under the weight of God's conviction.

First, there is *the absence of self-importance*. If you have a broken heart, you have no concept of your own importance. Any advantage you might feel over another is erased when you see yourself through the eyes of the omnipotent, holy God.

Second is *the absence of carelessness*. A broken and contrite heart has no room for frivolity and trifling. "A broken heart is serious, and solemn, and in earnest. A broken heart never tries to play any tricks with God, and never shuffles texts as though even Scripture itself were meant only to be an opportunity for testing our wit."

Third is *the absence of hypocrisy*. A broken heart cannot bear hypocrisy, especially within itself. After the trauma of conviction, it is particularly needy for reassurance, and only authenticity will do.

Fourth is *the absence of secrecy*. A broken heart cannot tolerate secrets. Secrecy has kept the guilty heart shrouded from intimacy with God and fellowship with others, the very things it was created to enjoy. Broken, contrite hearts are remarkably transparent, almost inappropriately so, perhaps because they have nothing more to hide.[8]

I concur with Spurgeon's comment, "When we remember [David's] sin, let us dwell most upon his penitence." Not everyone responds to confrontation and conviction as David did. Some will defend, justify, excuse, diminish the sinfulness of the sin, or lie to the bitter end. Many will grow hostile and attempt to discredit, or even destroy, their accusers. Without a doubt, David had this kind of power. But he did not abuse it. He was a man characterized by humility, which led him to repentance.

Humility welcomes criticism and willingly accepts responsibility for moral faults and human flaws. It seeks to learn from accusations, even unjust ones. Humility responds to failure with a sincere desire to grow, and sees itself as perpetually needy of divine forgiveness and empowerment.

HUMILITY IS GENTLE

Nathan had warned David, "The sword shall never depart from your house," and "Thus says the LORD, 'Behold, I will raise up evil against you from your own household; I will even take your wives before your eyes and give them to your companion, and he will lie with your wives in broad daylight'" (2 Samuel 12:10–11).

In time, chaos would tear the house of David into pieces. Amnon, David's eldest son, deceived and raped his half sister. In retaliation, David's son Absalom murdered Amnon, then fled Jerusalem to live with his maternal grandfather. David refused to interact with Absalom for several years before reluctantly allowing his son to return home. But by then, Absalom's resentment had eroded into full-blown hatred, which prompted him to solicit political support and lead an insurrection against his father. Before the rebellion was over, Absalom would fulfill the prophecy of Nathan by setting up a tent on the palace rooftop and shamelessly having sexual relations with David's concubines in full view of the nation.

Prior to this, when word reached David that Absalom was marching on Jerusalem, the king had only two choices: fight or flee. Humbly, the crushed king chose the latter. With no time to pack or to load animals, he, along with six hundred loyal troops and palace servants, fled Jerusalem on foot. They traveled down the eastern slope of

Jerusalem's mount, across the Kidron riverbed, and up the Mount of Olives. But before he got very far, he noticed the priests following with the ark of the covenant, the symbol of God's special, protective presence over Israel. His orders to them reveal that his heart was still tender several years after penning Psalm 51.

> The king said to [the chief priest], "Return the ark of God to the city. If I find favor in the sight of the LORD, then He will bring me back again and show me both it and His habitation. But if He should say thus, 'I have no delight in you,' behold, here I am, let Him do to me as seems good to Him." (2 Samuel 15:25–26)

David's humility had not faded; he understood the prophetic significance of the sad retreat from Jerusalem. He had no one to blame but himself. But I would stop short of calling this shame, not sensing depression or self-loathing. This is a man who is completely transparent about his faults, who has made his peace with God through repentance, and who enjoys a sweet intimacy with the Almighty because of grace. He is the same humble shepherd boy who, even after being anointed king, gladly tended sheep and polished armor. He is the same wilderness exile who never lost his right to rule Israel, yet left the matter in God's hands. Knowing he must endure the crushing consequences of his sin, he bypassed all thought of blame or retaliation.

Before David and his entourage traveled very far from Jerusalem, a demented relative of his predecessor, Saul, took the opportunity to kick the exiled king while he was down. Shimei ran along the hillside across from David and rained down dust and rocks with vile curses and insults. He shouted, "The LORD has returned upon you all the bloodshed of the house of Saul, in whose place you have reigned; and the LORD has given the kingdom into the hand of your son Absalom. And behold, you are taken in your own evil, for you are a man of bloodshed!" (2 Samuel 16:8).

One of David's generals offered to silence the old windbag by cutting off his head, something the king had every right to order. Yet David restrained his men. Though

Shimei was wrong in virtually everything he said, David accepted the rebuke as a natural consequence of his earlier failure, recognizing that so great a sin would have lasting and inescapable consequences. As far as he was concerned, the rebuke may or may not have been from the Lord, so he quietly resolved to allow God to deal with the man. The dust-hurling critic was never a danger to David's life, only his pride. But David's humility took the sting out of Shimei's assault.

When attacked by someone like the angry, deranged Shimei, you have two primary options. One is to stand toe-to-toe and exchange blows with your attacker. And, let's face it, that's our most natural response. Criticism is rarely fair and usually overblown. As David Roper writes:

- Criticism always comes when we least need it.

- Criticism seems to come when we least deserve it.

- Criticism comes from people who are least qualified to give it.

- Criticism frequently comes in a form that is least helpful to us.[9]

A second possible response to unfair criticism is to glean what truth we can. To quote a Yiddish proverb, "If one man calls you an ass, pay him no mind. If two men call you an ass, go buy a saddle." The criticism may be less than 50 percent accurate, but we are wise to sift it for anything that might be valid and then use it as an opportunity to address our wrongs.

"Make me into a rock which swallows up the waves of wrong in its great caverns and never throws them back to swell the commotion of the angry sea from whence they came. Ah! To annihilate wrong in this way—to say, 'It shall not be wrong against me, so utterly do I forgive it!'"[10]

— GEORGE MACDONALD

Humility chooses a gentle response to the petty hostility of critics. It is long-suffering, graceful, kind, even tender in the face of scorn. Humility returns good for evil, a soft answer in response to wrath, blessing for cursing, compassion for cruelty. Is it any wonder we called this a "rare virtue"?

HUMILITY RESTS
IN GOD'S SOVEREIGN CONTROL

David refused to defend himself against any attack on his pride because he was content to let any hint of pride be wiped out. Rather than take justice into his own hands, he left Shimei's reward or punishment in the hands of God. If David followed his usual practice, he took his frustration to the Lord in prayer. Psalm 109 was written in response to unfair verbal attacks and the slanderous plotting of enemies. Here's how David prayed:

- He stated the problem and called his enemies exactly what they were: liars and ingrates. (vv. 1–5)

- He asked the Lord for public vindication for himself and punishment for the wicked. (vv. 6–20)

- He looked to God for healing. (vv. 21–25)

- He found solace in the righteous sovereignty of God. (vv. 26–29)

- He praised the Lord for His faithfulness. (vv. 30–31)

A significant portion of David's prayer details his desire to see his enemies die an agonizing, humiliating death, to have their wives and children left destitute, to allow their lands to be pillaged or confiscated, and to curse their parents. He wanted to see his enemies so obliterated that even their memory would fade from people's minds! In other words, David took his passions out in the private safety of his relationship with the Lord. He didn't bottle them up or pretend that his outrage didn't exist; he expressed them in the appropriate context. And with his energies spent, he trusted that the Lord would receive his requests and then do what is right. "Let them curse, but You bless; / When they arise, they shall be ashamed, / But Your servant shall be glad" (v. 28).

While God, in His sovereign wisdom, permitted David's enemies to level their unwarranted assaults, He was also David's advocate. "For He stands at the right hand of the needy, / To save him from those who judge his soul" (v. 31).

Humility recognizes that God is in control of all circumstances—yes, *all*—and that all His ways—yes, *all*—are right. It never seeks vindication, choosing instead to allow the Lord to do the defending and justifying. Humility cares more about the Lord's good name than its own.

"You know to what extent You have already changed me, You who first healed me of the lust of vindicating myself, so that You might forgive all my remaining iniquities, and heal my diseases, and redeem my life from corruption, and crown me with loving-kindness and tender mercies, and satisfy my desire with good things."[11]

—St. Augustine

A Humble Benediction

We now have a better understanding of why the Lord expects us to walk humbly with Him. Pride is an insidious disease of the soul because it can turn even justice and kindness into self-righteous deeds. So, let me close this section with a prayer, a benediction for us all.

May we see pride as our archenemy and refuse its pleadings. Though it comes with utter reasonableness and soft entreaties, convincing appeals to our goodness and sense of worth, or even clever proof-texts from Holy Scripture, may we flee pride and heed the call of God to avoid thinking more of ourselves than we ought.

May we embrace humility as our closest friend and let things be. The world, once pristine and innocent, fell into sin and chaos shortly after the creation of people, and no amount of effort on our part will restore paradise. We cannot by our efforts right the wrongs of the world, even if we did possess flawless discernment. We must accept that we might be wrong more than we are right and find our rest in the Lord, allowing Him to correct others in His way . . . in His time.

May we return to the Cross when we find ourselves in need of an example of true humility. Proud, self-righteous men condemned Jesus to die. And proud, brutal men carried out the sentence. As they nailed Him to the cross and hung Him up there to die, He looked down with compassion and said, "Father, forgive them; for they do not know what they are doing" (Luke 23:34). His gentle, humble heart won the day. May He do so again with your heart and mine.

Chapter 4

Enjoying the Rewards

WHAT DOES THE LORD EXPECT OF US? "TO DO justice, to love kindness, and to walk humbly with your God." Peter and John relentlessly pursued justice by doing what was right. Joseph's love for kindness can be seen in the tender forgiveness he extended to his treacherous brothers. David walked humbly with God through triumph and failure, and the Lord called the shepherd-king a man after His own heart. Three remarkable examples of what it means to live well. And, best of all, their stories are real. No fables here. No image crafting. Though not perfect, they did what was right, loved kindness, and walked humbly with God . . . *authentically*. What we know of them after their deaths is no different than what everyone knew of them in life. And that makes them heroes.

All of us need heroes to inspire and challenge us. And it may surprise you to know that, someday, you might be someone's hero. You might be the example that your child or grandchild looks to for inspiration. That may seem unlikely to you because all you see are your flaws. Interestingly, though, we don't seek perfection in our heroes. It's *authenticity* we crave.

Authenticity makes the reward of a life well lived transferable to others.

The Need for Integrity

Authenticity is a product of integrity, which the dictionary defines as "an unimpaired condition, wholeness, completeness, soundness." It's based on the root word *integer*, which means "untouched, intact, entire." A person with integrity is not divided (that's *duplicity*) or devious (that's *deception*) or merely pretending (that's *hypocrisy*). People with integrity have nothing to hide and nothing to fear. Their lives are transparent. Though, unfortunately, they are also somewhat rare.

Several years ago James Patterson and Peter Kim released a penetrating book that shocked many in our country. The two men unveiled the results of an extensive opinion survey in which the anonymity of its participants was guaranteed. They titled their report *The Day America Told the Truth*. This two-hundred-plus page volume exposed the integrity crisis our country faced—a shortage we continue to endure. For example, they reported:

- Only 13 percent of Americans see all Ten Commandments as binding and relevant.[12]

- No less than 91 percent lie regularly, both at work and in their homes.[13]

- Most Americans admit to "goofing off" for an average of seven hours per week, and half our workforce admits that they regularly call in sick when they feel perfectly well.[14]

The answers to one particular question sent shivers down my spine: "What are you willing to do for $10 million?"

- 25 percent would abandon their families

- 23 percent would become a prostitute for a week

- 7 percent would murder a stranger[15]

Pause to think about that last one. In a random gathering of one hundred Americans, seven would consider murdering you if the price were right. In a group of a thousand, that's *seventy* potential murderers!

And before you start feeling a little smug as a Christian, perhaps thinking that our ranks are filled with only the pure of heart, don't go there too quickly. In another published work, *Keeping Your Ethical Edge Sharp*, two other authors, Doug Sherman and William Hendricks (both of them Christians), built an embarrassing case against the Christian community using undeniable, hard evidence. They came to the conclusion that "the general ethical conduct of Christians varies only slightly from non-Christians." They found that Christians are just as likely to:

- Falsify their income tax returns

- Lie to their employers about being sick

- Bribe to obtain a building permit

- Steal from the workplace

- Selectively obey the laws[16]

Before you shake your head and cluck your tongue, do a deep-level search of your own heart. Do *you* do any of those things? If someone offered *you* $10 million with a few ethical strings attached, could you be bought? How much does your integrity cost?

Elton Trueblood underscores an essential quality he calls "the moral element":

> It is hard to think of any job in which the moral element is lacking. The skill of the dentist is wholly irrelevant, if he is unprincipled and irresponsible. There is little, in that case, to keep him from withdrawing teeth unnecessarily, because the patient is usually in a helpless situation. It is easy to see the harm that can be done by an unprincipled lawyer. Indeed, such a person is far more dangerous if he is skilled than if he is unskilled.[17]

In *Boardroom Reports*, Peter LeVine writes, "When the Port Authority of New York and New Jersey ran a help-wanted ad for electricians with expertise at using Sontag connectors, it got 170 responses—even though there is *no such thing* as a Sontag connector."[18] The Authority ran the ad to find out how many applicants falsify résumés.

A MAN YOU COULD TRUST

With so many examples of questionable character, we could begin to believe that there is no one we can trust . . . no one who keeps his word or walks the talk. Not true. Every era in history has had a remnant of righteous men and women who avoided the moral quicksand of their age. Unlike many of their peers, their integrity kept them from drowning in swamps of ethical compromise.

Centuries ago there lived such a man; his name was Daniel.

Daniel was a Hebrew who had been taken captive by the Babylonians after they had brutally invaded the land of Judah, destroyed its cities, and obliterated the Jewish temple. Thousands of Jewish exiles were forced from their native soil to be settled in a foreign land where they would be immersed in a corrupt culture that was characterized by paganism and idolatry. Through a series of remarkable decisions and events, Daniel's integrity kept him free of contamination while at the same time cultivating the trust of his pagan superiors. In fact, he went from serving one godless monarch to another and yet another, all the while earning their respect and receiving increased authority. He was a powerful leader in two world empires, which made him the target of many attacks by envious political enemies. Daniel 6 records one such conspiracy.

At this point in his biography, Daniel had been a well-known figure in the Babylonian government for many decades, and he was about to receive a new appointment under the new Medo-Persian Empire. Eugene Peterson's *The Message* paraphrases the scriptural account this way:

Darius reorganized his kingdom. He appointed one hundred twenty governors to administer all the parts of his realm. Over them were three vice-regents, one of whom was Daniel. The governors reported to the vice-regents, who made sure that everything was in order for the king. But Daniel, brimming with spirit and intelligence, so completely outclassed the other vice-regents and governors that the king decided to put him in charge of the whole kingdom.

The vice-regents and governors got together to find some old scandal or skeleton in Daniel's life that they could use against him, but they couldn't dig up anything. He was totally exemplary and trustworthy. They could find no evidence of negligence or misconduct. So they finally gave up and said, "We're never going to find anything against this Daniel unless we can cook up something religious." (vv. 1–5 MSG)

To gain some appreciation for this, imagine arriving at your place of business one morning to find a 60 *Minutes* film crew at the front door. As the cameras roll, reporters and government officials rifle through your files, probe your computer, scrutinize your financial records, and evaluate your business dealings over the past several years, all in a desperate hope of finding some dirt they can expose and exploit. For Daniel, the investigation was not merely invasive and prejudiced, it was led by a group of men who were determined to find something—anything!—against him. But they found nothing. In the words of the Bible, "They could find no ground of accusation or evidence of corruption, inasmuch as he was faithful" (v. 6:4).

What a model of integrity! He lived life well and he lived it openly. In fact, this is the same Daniel of the famed lions' den. Remember the Sunday school story? His enemies couldn't find any skeletons, so they concocted a law they knew he would break: a law against praying to anyone other than the king. When the law passed, Daniel did as he had always done. He threw open the windows that faced Jerusalem, and he prayed.

His integrity produced a transparent existence, a life characterized by authenticity.

THE REWARDS OF A LIFE WELL LIVED

A life well lived honors the Lord and inspires others, but it also produces rewards for the one who lives it. At least six are significant enough to mention.

First, the sustained cultivation of exemplary character.

Day after day, year after year, the one who commits himself or herself to the pursuit of justice, kindness, and humility will most certainly develop strong character. And it won't be merely a façade. It will be the same bone-deep beauty that drew people to Jesus Christ during His early sojourn, the same quality of spirit that inspired God the Father to say, "This is My beloved Son, with whom I am well . . . pleased" (Matthew 17:5).

Second, the continued relief of a clear conscience.

Who hasn't tossed and turned, fretted and struggled through a night filled with feelings of guilt? The voice of our conscience is eloquent . . . and convincing . . . and strong. It refuses to be silenced when we know that we have compromised where integrity said we should not. When we doggedly do what is right, when we generously give kindness, and when we remain intimate with God, our conscience remains free of any nagging emotional aches. A clear conscience gives relief, relief grants freedom, freedom inspires joy, and joy bears the fruit of a robust sense of humor.

Third, the personal delight of intimacy with the Almighty.

As author Dr. Kent Hughes has stated so aptly, "A transparent soul is a haven for the Spirit of God." God is still seeking those whose hearts are fully committed to Him—His will, His way, His Word. One way we can get to know someone is to walk a mile in his shoes. To do what the Lord expects of us is to honor His values and do as His Son did. And in this way, we grow in our intimacy with Him.

Fourth, the high privilege of being a mentor.

It is one thing to be a teacher and leader for others, but quite another to be a mentor—someone who has earned the right to become a trusted counselor, a personal coach and guide who plays a significant role in shaping another's life. Heroes, as crucial as they are, generally live at a distance—some have even died. But a mentor is someone who lives up close and personal, providing hands-on guidance, correction, and affirmation in face-to-face encounters. Mentors don't typically apply for the job, nor do they pass a series of tests in order to qualify for the role. Mentors are chosen based on observation. A life well lived allows us the privilege of positively impacting another life.

Fifth, the crowning reward of finishing well.

As we grow older, one haunting thought that once lingered in the back of our minds begins to dominate all others. It's the fear of approaching the end of our lives beaten down, beached, and broken. T. S. Eliot expressed the fear well in his work, "This is the way the world ends / Not with a bang but a whimper."[19]

I cannot think of a more dreadful thought. But the possibility of that kind of end exists, even for one who has been actively and productively engaged throughout his or her entire adult life. Even for one as influential and spiritual as the apostle Paul, the thought of finishing his life "disqualified" was neither imaginary nor remote (1 Corinthians 9:27). Fortunately, those who continue along the path of a life well lived will not only gain the pleasure of spending their years in a worthy pursuit; they will also enjoy the crowning reward of finishing well.

Sixth, a priceless, lingering legacy for those we love.

Those who fret over their legacy have revealed themselves to be shallow, superficial people. When we do what is right, love kindness, and stay close to God, the natural product will be a lingering legacy by which *anybody* would want to be remembered. Live well now and you will continue to live well in the memories of the people you value. A life lived as described in these pages will never be forgotten. Just think, long after you have passed from this earth, you will continue to speak!

THE ULTIMATE GIFT OF A LIFE WELL LIVED

I have a good friend named Bob, who comes from a large, closely knit Italian family. The shadow of his father's life of goodness and uncompromising integrity spread across each one of the children from their birth until his death, which came late in life. Bob has nothing but pleasant memories of being with his father, listening to his stories, watching him endure numerous trials, laughing and lingering around the supper table, and observing his tender, affectionate relationship with his wife of many decades. He was clearly the leader of his home—decisive, fair, kind, humble, joyful, and pure. Frankly, Bob thought him almost too good to be true.

Without warning, Bob's wonderful father died. Even though all the children were grown and on their own, the jolt of his being gone was almost more than the family could manage. Their grief ran deep as tears flowed and hearts broke. After the funeral, it was necessary for all of them to deal with the practical matters of carrying on, which included those difficult tasks of disposing of the man's clothing, wrapping up his financial affairs, and sifting through the remainder of his personal effects to be certain everything was resolved. All those tasks were shared by various members of the family . . . and Bob was chosen to handle that last responsibility. He would be the one to sit down and look through things that other eyes had never seen—not even the man's wife, Bob's mother.

As you can imagine, Bob was reluctant. Fear gripped him as he wondered what scandal or dishonor he might find. Would he uncover some secret sin? Would he find evidence of moral compromise? Would the man's computer reveal some questionable sites he had frequently visited? Would there be invoices he'd never paid, traffic tickets he'd ignored and buried from view, or worse, a picture or love note from a mystery woman? Bob dreaded the thought of *anything* tarnishing the image of the man who had been not only a marvelous father but his hero, his mentor, and his model for life.

Though reluctant and fearful, Bob accepted the task, and with diligent, cautious concern, he dug in. Hour after hour, all alone, he silently examined his deceased father's personal belongings. He read journal entries, looked through dozens of photographs, examined financial records, thumbed through stacks of handwritten notes, unlocked private areas of the man's Internet activities, and read letters he had written and received. Bob eventually discovered his father's most personal little boxes and sealed envelopes, which he thoroughly searched, examining every file, every folder.

Meticulously and tediously, Bob searched through it all. And to his great delight, he found nothing that was even near questionable or suspicious. *Nothing.* The man was as clear and clean in his private life as he had been before his family and in the eyes of the public—a modern-day Daniel, "who was faithful . . . no negligence or corruption was found in him" (Daniel 6:4).

Bob wept audibly. The man he had admired all his life was everything he had believed him to be.

This is the greatest reward of a life well lived.

He has told you, O man, what is good;
And what does the LORD require of you
But to do justice, to love kindness,
And to walk humbly with your God?

—MICAH 6:8

Notes

1. *Merriam-Webster's Collegiate Dictionary*, 10th ed., s.v. "kind."

2. Henry George Liddell and Robert Scott, *A Greek-English Lexicon*, rev. ed. (Oxford: Clarendon Press, 1968), 2007.

3. Brennan Manning, *Abba's Child* (Colorado Springs: NavPress, 2002), 72–73.

4. Ken Gire, *A Father's Gift: The Legacy of Memories* (Grand Rapids: Zondervan Publishing House, 1992), 51–53, 57.

5. Jess Moody, *A Drink at Joel's Place* (Waco, TX: Word Books, 1967), 45–46.

6. Reprinted from *The Root of Righteousness* by A. W. Tozer, Copyright © 1986 by Zur Ltd. Used by permission of WingSpread Publishers, a division of Zur Ltd., 800-884-4571.

7. C. H. Spurgeon, *The Treasury of David*, Vol. 2 (New York: Funk & Wagnalls Company, 1881), 29.

8. C. H. Spurgeon, *The Metropolitan Tabernacle Pulpit*, Vol. 41 (Pasadena, TX: Pilgrim Publications, 1975), 303–4.

9. David Roper, *A Burden Shared: Encouragement for Leaders* (Grand Rapids: Discovery House Publishers, 1991), 59.

10. George MacDonald, quoted in Roper, *A Burden Shared*, 61.

11. St. Augustine, *The Confessions of St. Augustine*, Book X, Chapter 36, in *Everyman's Library: Theology and Philosophy*, ed. Ernest Rhys (London: J. M. Dent & Sons, 1936), 241.

12. James Patterson and Peter Kim, *The Day America Told the Truth: What People Really Believe about Everything That Really Matters* (New York: Prentice Hall Press, 1991), cover.

13. Ibid.

14. Ibid.

15. Ibid.

16. Doug Sherman and William Hendricks, *Keeping Your Ethical Edge Sharp: How to Cultivate a Personal Character that Is Honest, Faithful, Just, and Morally Clean* (Colorado Springs: NavPress, 1990), 30.

17. Elton Trueblood, *Your Other Vocation* (New York: Harper & Brothers, 1952), 74.

18. Peter LeVine, *Boardroom Reports*, July 15, 1993, quoted in Leadership, Vol. 15, No. 1, Winter 1994, 47.

19. T.S. Eliot, *The Complete Poems and Plays*, 1909–1950 (New York: Harcourt Brace & Company, 1980), 59.

About the Author

CHARLES R. SWINDOLL IS SENIOR PASTOR OF Stonebriar Community Church, Chancellor of Dallas Theological Seminary, and host of the internationally syndicated radio program Insight for Living. He has written more than thirty best-selling books, such as *Strengthening Your Grip*, *Laugh Again*, and the Great Lives series, including *Paul: A Man of Grace and Grit*. Chuck and his wife, Cynthia, live in Frisco, Texas.

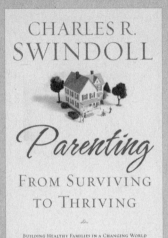

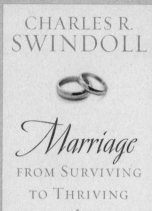

Building a Biblical Marriage

Best-selling author Charles R. Swindoll uses his warm, humorous yet always insightful writing style to bring some much needed advice on the subject of marriage. Drawing from his own personal experience with Cynthia, his wife of 50 years, as well as showing what the Bible says about marriage, Charles will give very practical and inspiring ways to building a marriage that not only thrives but survives the tests of time.

Workbook also available

INSIGHT FOR LIVING

THOMAS NELSON
Since 1798

For other products and live events,
visit us at: thomasnelson.com

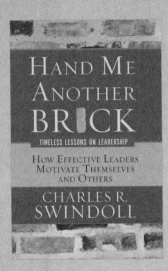

Lessons in Leadership

Most of us could benefit from wise advice on how to be a more effective leader at work *and* at home. In this revised edition, Charles Swindoll delves deep into the life of Nehemiah to show how to handle with integrity the issues of motivation, discouragement, and adversity.

Bible Companion also available

INSIGHT FOR LIVING

THOMAS NELSON
Since 1798

For other products and live events,
visit us at: thomasnelson.com

The
Great Lives Series
Continues

This next installment of the Great Lives series unveils the life of Jesus and reinspires with insight, teaching, and historical information that strengthens not only a person's belief and awe of the Savior but also their understanding of his life and teaching.

Great Lives: Jesus — Available Now

Jesus Bible Companion
also available

THOMAS NELSON
Since 1798

INSIGHT FOR LIVING

For other products and live events,
visit us at: **thomasnelson.com**

Daily Insight ... for Living Life Well

"God looks beneath and beyond all outward expressions of religious devotion to examine our character. What honors the Lord is a heart that beats in the same rhythm as His, a spirit that values the same qualities that define Him. He wants people who do what is right, who love kindness, and who walk humbly with Him."

— CHARLES R. SWINDOLL

Insight for Living, the Bible-teaching radio ministry of Charles R. Swindoll, seeks to help people develop an authentic relationship with the Lord and enjoy the rewards of a life well lived. The daily broadcast can be heard on more than 2,000 radio stations around the world, on the Internet, and via podcasting.

Visit **www.insight.org** to discover how you can begin receiving practical teaching from God's Word—daily insights to help you live well.

INSIGHT FOR LIVING

THOMAS NELSON
Since 1798

For other products and live events,
visit us at: **thomasnelson.com**